Insect World
Ladybugs

by Mari Schuh

Bullfrog
Books

Ideas for Parents and Teachers

Bullfrog Books let children practice nonfiction reading at the earliest reading levels. Repetition, familiar words, and photo labels support early readers.

Before Reading

- Discuss the cover photo. What does it tell them?
- Look at the picture glossary together. Read and discuss the words.

Read the Book

- "Walk" through the book and look at the photos. Let the child ask questions. Point out the photo labels.
- Read the book to the child, or have him or her read independently.

After Reading

- Prompt the child to think more. Ask: Have you ever seen a ladybug? Was it eating something? How did it move?

The author dedicates this book to Cami and Avery Schuh of Mankato, Minnesota.

Bullfrog Books are published by Jump!
5357 Penn Avenue South
Minneapolis, MN 55419
www.jumplibrary.com

Library of Congress Cataloging-in-Publication Data
Schuh, Mari C., 1975-
Ladybugs / by Mari Schuh.
p. cm. -- (Insect world)
Summary: "This photo-illustrated book for early readers tells facts about ladybugs and briefly explains their life cycle. Includes picture glossary" --Provided by publisher.
ISBN 978-1-62031-055-7 (hardcover : alk. paper)
-- ISBN 1-62031-055-4 (hardcover : alk. paper) --
ISBN 978-1-62496-047-5 (ebook) -- ISBN 1-62496-047-2 (ebook)
1. Ladybugs--Juvenile literature. 2. Ladybugs--Life cycles--Juvenile literature. I. Title. II. Series: Schuh, Mari C., 1975- Insect world.
QL596.C65 S36 2014
595.76'9--dc23   2012039941

Series Editor   Rebecca Glaser
Book Designer   Ellen Huber
Photo Researcher   Heather Dreisbach

Photo Credits: 123rf, 22; Alamy, 15; Bigstock 3, 22; Biosphoto, 16; Corbis, 6, 21, 23tr; iStock, 1, 18–19, 23bl; Shutterstock, cover, 4, 7, 9, 10-11, 13–14, 23tl, 23ml; Superstock, 8, 17, 20, 23br; Veer, 5, 12, 23mr, 24

Printed in the United States of America at Corporate Graphics in North Mankato, Minnesota.
4-2013 / P.O. 1003

10 9 8 7 6 5 4 3 2 1

Table of Contents

Hungry Ladybugs

Look at the big leaf.
What is round and red?

It is a ladybug.

Ladybugs help farmers.

They eat aphids.

Aphids hurt crops.

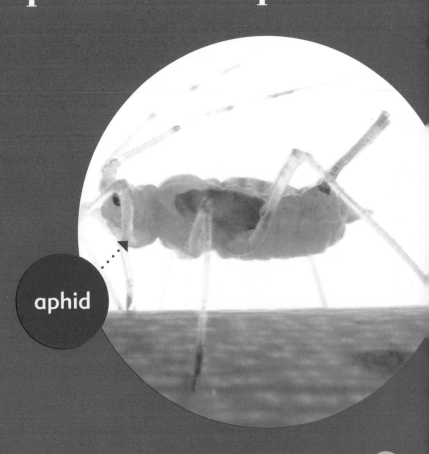

aphid

Chomp! Chomp!
Ladybugs
are big eaters.

8

They can eat 5,000 aphids in a few weeks.

Look out!
A bird is hungry.

He wants to
eat a ladybug.

The ladybug plays dead.

The bird flies away.
The ladybug is safe.

eggs

Ladybugs lay eggs.

Larvas hatch.

They eat and eat.

larva

The larvas grow.
They shed their
skin a few times.

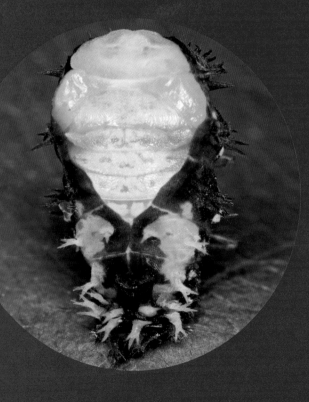

pupa

Now they are pupas.
They change into ladybugs.

swarm

Winter comes.

The ladybugs do
not eat in winter.

They hibernate.

They sleep in
big groups
called swarms.

It is spring.

The ladybugs
wake up.

They eat
more bugs.

Chomp! Chomp!

Parts of a Ladybug

antenna
A short feeler that a ladybug uses to smell and feel.

leg
A ladybug has six legs, like all insects.

hard wings
Two strong wings that protect a ladybug's soft wings.

soft wings
Two wings that a ladybug uses to fly.

Picture Glossary

aphid
A tiny insect with a soft body that eats plants.

larva
A young ladybug that hatches from an egg; it does not have wings.

crops
Plants such as corn or wheat that are grown in large amounts for food.

play dead
To stay still and pretend to be dead so that enemies go away.

hibernate
To spend winter in a deep sleep.

pupa
The third stage of a ladybug's life; pupas change into adult ladybugs.

Index

To Learn More

Learning more is as easy as 1, 2, 3.

1) Go to www.factsurfer.com

2) Enter "ladybug" into the search box.

3) Click the "Surf" button to see a list of websites.

With factsurfer.com, finding more information is just a click away.